ROBBIE BYERLY

# Rainforests

A rainforest can have water.

A rainforest can have waterfalls.

A rainforest can have mountains.

A rainforest can have rocks.

A rainforest can have trees.

6

A rainforest can have flowers.

A rainforest can have leaves.

A rainforest can have plants.

A rainforest can have tigers.

A rainforest can have monkeys.

11

A rainforest can have birds.

A rainforest can have snakes.

A rainforest can have lizards.

A rainforest can have frogs.

A rainforest can have spiders.

A rainforest can have bugs.

A rainforest can have butterflies.

18

# Power Words

**How many can you read?**

A

a

can

have

# I can match the word to the picture using the first letter sound.

rocks

frog

water

tiger